# SHEET MUSIC *for* PIANO

# Rachmaninov

## Intermediate to Advanced Piano Masterpieces

MP3s
ONLINE LINKS
Resources

## Alan Brown

### With an Introduction by Sarah Gabriel

## FLAME TREE PUBLISHING

FLAME TREE
PIANO KEYBOARD

Publisher and Creative Director: Nick Wells
Project Editor: Polly Prior
Music Transcription: Alan Brown
Introductory Text: Sarah Gabriel

This edition first published 2015 by
FLAME TREE PUBLISHING
Crabtree Hall, Crabtree Lane
Fulham, London SW6 6TY
United Kingdom
www.flametreepublishing.com
www.flametreemusic.com

**Website for this book: www.flametreepiano.com**

© 2015 Flame Tree Publishing Ltd

15 17 19 18 16
1 3 5 7 9 10 8 6 4 2

ISBN 978-1-78361-425-7

A CIP record for this book is available from the British Library upon request.

**Alan Brown (Music Transcription)**
A former member of the Scottish National Orchestra, Alan now works as a freelance
musician, with several leading UK orchestras, and as a consultant in music and IT. Alan has
had several compositions published, developed a set of music theory CD-Roms, co-written a
series of Bass Guitar Examination Handbooks and worked on over 100 further titles.

**Sarah Gabriel (Introductory Text)**
Sarah Gabriel is a singer and actor. She made her USA debut conducted by Lorin Maazel
and her European debut as Eliza in *My Fair Lady* at Théâtre de Châtelet, Paris. Passionate
about song, she has given recitals across Europe, the US and Asia, and in the UK at festivals
and venues such as Glyndebourne, Cheltenham International Festival and Wigmore Hall.

Printed in China

# Contents

# How to Use the Website

The Flame Tree Piano and Keyboard website (www.flametreepiano.com) offers a number of significant benefits for readers and users of this sheet music book. It can be accessed on a desktop computer (Mac or PC), tablet (such as the iPad or Nexus) or any internet enabled smartphone.

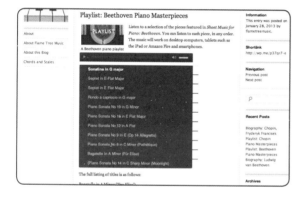

## The Home Page

With a series of options the website allows the reader to find out more, both about the composer and the music. Biographies, mp3s and further resources are provided to allow you to explore the subject further.

## The Audio Player

The primary tool on the website is the use of an audio player. All the pieces are presented to help you understand each of the masterpieces in this book. The simple play ▶ button allows you to play each piece through the speakers on your device. Although the music cannot be downloaded it is streamed, and is provided free of charge.

## Life and Works

This book of sheet music pieces for the piano is introduced with a short guide to the composer. The website presents a more extensive text on the life, works, style and context, with information extracted from *The Classical Music Encyclopedia* (Flame Tree Publishing), edited by Stanley Sadie

(1930–2005), with a foreword by Vladimir Ashkenazy. Music editor for *The Times* for 17 years and editor of the standard classical music reference work *The New Grove Dictionary of Music and Musicians*, Stanley Sadie was, amongst many other achievements, president of the Royal Musical Association and the International Musicological Society. (*The Classical Music Encyclopedia* will be republished online and made available as a downloadable pdf, from www.flametreepiano.com.)

## Free eBook

Created to complement this new series of books we have made a special edition, 96 page ebook, *Romantic Composers*. Featuring the primary composers, musicians and musical artists of the Romantic Era, the ebook can be downloaded onto any computer, tablet or smartphone and is an invaluable source of reference on a key period of musical history.

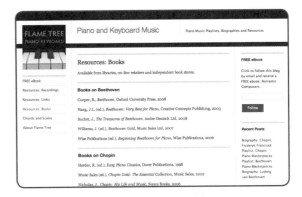

## Other Features

The experience of playing the piano is one of constant development. To help with further discoveries we have provided a number of additional resources. Separate menus offer recommendations for further reading (books and online) and particular recordings.

# Introduction to Rachmaninov

**THE MUSICAL VOICE of Sergey Vasilyevich Rachmaninov (1873–1943) is instantly recognizable, and much loved for its unabashed lyricism and romantic expression.** His reputation as a composer is inseparable from the works that he wrote for piano. As an exceptional pianist he exploited fully the capabilities of the instrument, and many of his recordings are still appreciated as seminal interpretations of his own and others' compositions.

His piano works such as the Twenty-Four Preludes, *Etudes-Tableaux*, *Moments Musicaux* and concertos are evidently influenced by the European Romantics, including Schumann, Chopin and Liszt, and yet there is a strikingly individual voice to his undulating, expansive and extended melodies. What began as a rather nationalistic Russian sound in his early years as a composer became a distinctive and often introspective musical language that was uniquely his own, inspiring to many and often imitated since. As well as being standard repertoire in classical concert halls across the world, his music has been adopted with ease by Western popular culture, from iconic films (such as *Brief Encounter*) to chart music.

## Critical Disdain

Rachmaninov's work is not without its detractors. Eric Blom wrote in the 1954 edition of *Grove Dictionary of Music and Musicians* that 'technically he was highly gifted' but that his music is 'monotonous' in texture, consisting 'mainly of artificial and gushing tunes accompanied by a variety of figures derived from arpeggios'. He asserted that Rachmaninov's huge popular acclaim 'is not likely to last, and musicians never regarded it with much favour'. Rachmaninov almost disappeared from a number of musical encyclopaedias in the twentieth century – seemingly a mark of disdain for his popularity and accessibility. However, his legacy endures and continues to thrive.

## Indigence, Indolence, Excellence

Born on an estate near Great Novgorod in north-western Russia into a family that was both military and musical, Rachmaninov would have been destined for a career as an army officer had his feckless father managed to conserve some of their wealth. Instead, his womanising and profligacy caught up with him, and he eventually abandoned his wife and six children. The young Sergey's mother gave him his first music lessons, during which he showed great promise, and then a piano teacher, Anna Ornatskaya, was brought in from St Petersburg in 1882 to formalize his studies. As the family continued to suffer a decline in its fortunes, Rachmaninov's grandmother supported his musical development, as well as his spiritual upbringing.

He began studying at the St Petersburg Conservatory in 1882 at the age of 10, where he became so unable to apply himself to his work that he failed his general studies. In his autobiography, Rimsky-Korsakov wrote of this period of Rachmaninov's childhood as one of 'purely Russian self-delusion and laziness', although this desultory academic performance may actually have been an early effect of the depression that was to affect the composer throughout his life.

Despite Rachmaninov's inauspicious beginnings at St Petersburg, frantic negotiations and family connections ensured that he was awarded a place at the Moscow Conservatory, where he was subjected to a strict practice regime under the watchful eye of the piano professor Zverev, starting work each morning at six o'clock. From the age of sixteen he also studied composition with Arensky and Taneyev (his counterpoint teacher under the advice of Tchaikovsky). It was during this time of focused study that Rachmaninov also learned that he could only compose in total seclusion, which remained the case for the rest of his life. He graduated with the rarely and unanimously-awarded Great Gold Medal in 1892.

## From Graduation to Freedom

This great accolade, and the acceptance of the winning piece (his one-act opera Aleko) for production by the Bolshoi, gave Rachmaninov an initial period of liberation in which he was now entitled to call himself a 'Free Artist'. That same year, he also composed *Morceaux de Fantaisie (Op. 3)*, a set of five piano pieces that included his famous Prelude in C Sharp Minor. A few orchestral pieces, further works for piano and a number of songs followed that year.

This productive period was undoubtedly clouded by the death of Tchaikovsky on 6 November 1893. On the very same day, Rachmaninov began his *Trio Élégiaque*, and the dark shadows in this piece indicate the depth of his distress. '[His death] was a great blow to me,' he wrote later in his *Recollections*, 'I lost not only a fatherly friend who had set me an example as a musician... [but also] a loyal supporter and faithful adviser who I needed badly for my first faltering steps in the world of music.'

## Stumbling Towards Success

In 1897, the première of his *First Symphony in D minor* (which included motifs redolent of his childhood on his grandmother's estate in Novgorod) had a disastrous reception. There were rumours that Glazunov, who conducted the premiere, had been drunk, but Rachmaninov had also rejected Taneyev's advice to edit the piece, feeling unable to change work that was so personal. Devastated and depressed at the critical response, he stopped composing for three years.

During this time, he nonetheless established himself as an international performer, with engagements that included playing the piano and conducting his own orchestral works in London in 1899. Thus began a pattern that reappeared throughout his life: the burden – and financial strain – of feeling unable to compose for significant periods of time ensured that his performing often took priority.

Once Rachmaninov felt able to return to composing he completed his celebrated Second Piano Concerto in 1901, the same year that he wrote his Cello Sonata. He married his first cousin, Natalya Satina, in 1902, and the following year the first of their two daughters, Irina, was born.

This period brought various successes as a conductor, pianist and composer, but the 1905 Revolution precipitated Rachmaninov's first self-imposed exile. He left his job as conductor of the Bolshoi and moved to Dresden in November 1906, where he composed his second symphony, *The Isle of the Dead* (a symphonic poem) and the highly virtuosic Piano Concerto No. 3 in D Minor. This became a hugely successful calling card in the United States when he debuted as a pianist with the New York Symphony in 1909, followed by a triumphant tour to Philadelphia and Chicago as conductor. In 1910, he returned to Russia, despite an invitation to become the resident conductor at Boston Symphony.

His composing over the following years was aided by the isolation of his country retreat, Ivanovka (which originally belonged to his wife's family). His choral symphony, *The Bells*, written in 1913, while certainly not radical, was nonetheless texturally innovative. His *All-Night Vigil* (1915), deeply embedded in the Russian choral tradition, demonstrated the same profound understanding of the human voice as his solo songs, the last of which he wrote in 1916. By 1917 his reputation as his country's most notable conductor and an important composer was established, but also under imminent threat.

## Upheaval and Exile

After the October Revolution of 1917 Rachmaninov's background meant that he was of the wrong social class to thrive as a musician under the new Russian regime. He felt it necessary to leave his country, which he did so in December that year. After a brief stay in Stockholm and Copenhagen, he and his family immigrated to America at the end of 1918. He never returned to Russia and, it has often been claimed, never quite recovered.

In 1931, despite his fourteen-year absence from Russia, his musical influence was still considered to be sufficiently subversive that an official Soviet verdict was issued, stating that Rachmaninov's music was 'especially dangerous on the musical front in the present class war.'

## A Pragmatic Decision to Perform

Once in the United States, his concert work took precedence, along with his legendary studio recording work. Possessed of an excellent memory (at the age of 15 he had played Glazunov's Fifth Symphony on the piano after one hearing) Rachmaninov was able to establish a broad repertoire as a performer.

He found a kindred spirit in Vladimir Horowitz when they met in 1928. Both Russian émigrés whose lives had changed with the revolution, they performed together frequently and remained friends for life. Horowitz's interpretation of the Third Piano Concerto was met with particular acclaim.

Alongside his intensive concert schedule, Rachmaninov composed his Fourth Piano Concerto (1926), the ebullient *Rhapsody on a Theme by Paganini* (1934), the *Third Symphony* (1938) and *Symphonic Dances* (1940). However, his pace of composing suffered – partly because of his busy performance calendar, but also because of his profound homesickness for Russia. Following his arrival in the USA in 1918, he wrote only six pieces until his death (from melanoma, four days short of his seventieth birthday and less than two months after becoming an American citizen) in 1943.

## Against the New Musical Tide

Rachmaninov lived and composed in a time of universal tumult, through revolution in Russia and two world wars. Many of his contemporaries responded to the horrors of the early twentieth century with new musical forms: atonality and serialism, striking angular rhythms, experimental instrumentation and orchestration. But Rachmaninov was sceptical about the approach of many modernists to musical expression, as he explained in an interview in 1941: 'I can respect the artistic aim of a composer if he arrives at the so-called modern idiom after an intense period of preparation... [but] too much radical music is sheer sham, for this very reason: its composer sets about revolutionizing the laws of music before he has learned them himself.'

He continued defiantly to reside in the realm of tonality. Though often labelled 'conservative' for its romanticism in a modern age, Rachmaninov's music has deservedly won enduring recognition for its rich legacy. As Michael Kennedy notes in *The Concise Oxford Dictionary of Music*, 'He was the last of the colourful Russian masters of the late 19th century, with their characteristic gift for long and broad melodies imbued with a resigned melancholy which is never long absent.'

11

# Barcarolle
## (Op 10, No. 3 in G Minor)

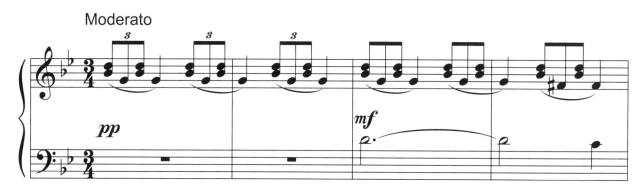

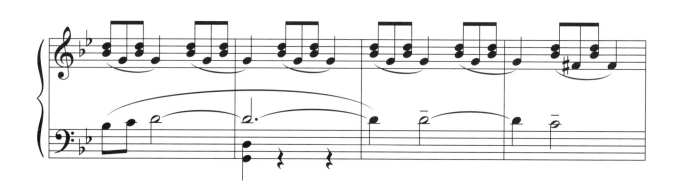

Con moto

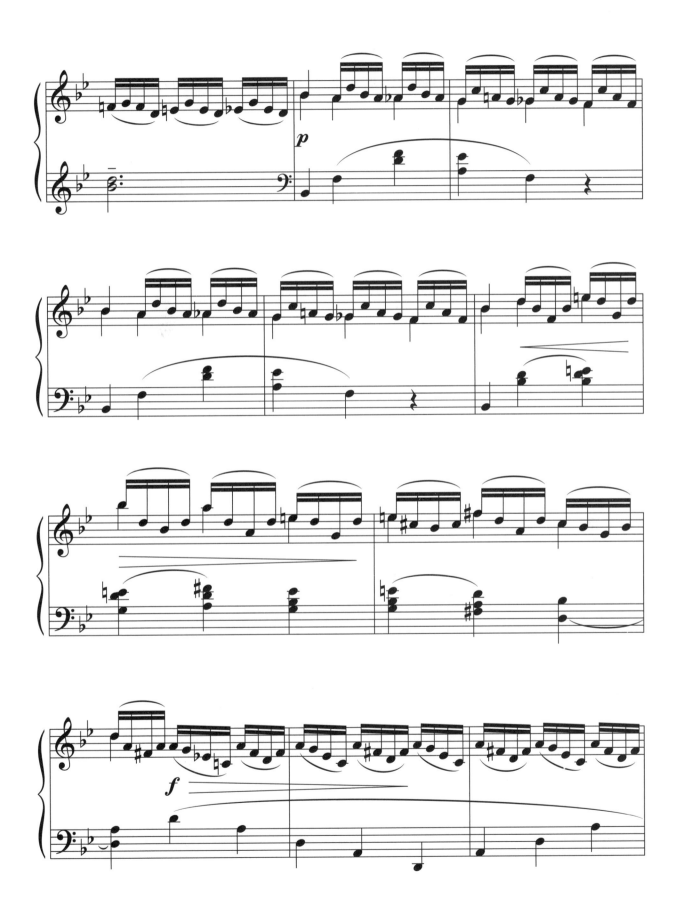

Allegro moderato

Meno mosso

Con moto

# Études-Tableaux
## (Op 33, No. 2 in C Major)

Allegro

# Études-Tableaux
## (Op 33, No. 6 in E Flat Major)

Allegro con fuoco

# Études-Tableaux
## (Op. 39, No. 2 in A Minor)

Lento assai

# Melodie

## (Op 3, No. 3 in E Major)

Adagio sostenuto

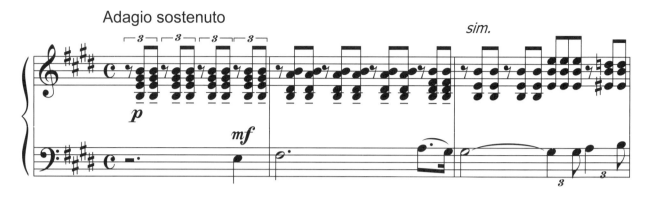

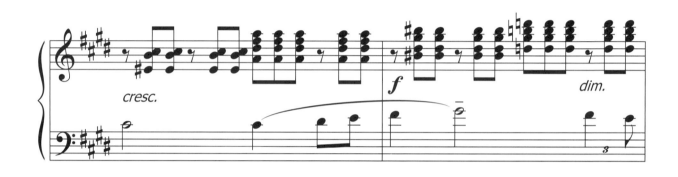

# Moments musicaux

## (Op. 16, No. 3 in B minor)

# Moments musicaux
## (Op. 16, No. 5 in D Flat Major)

Adagio sostenuto

# Polichinelle

## (Op 3, No. 4 in F Sharp Minor)

Allegro vivace

# Prelude in B Major

## (Op 32, No. 11)

# Prelude in D Major

## (Op 23, No. 4)

Andante cantabile

# Prelude in E Flat Major
## (Op 23, No. 6)

Andante

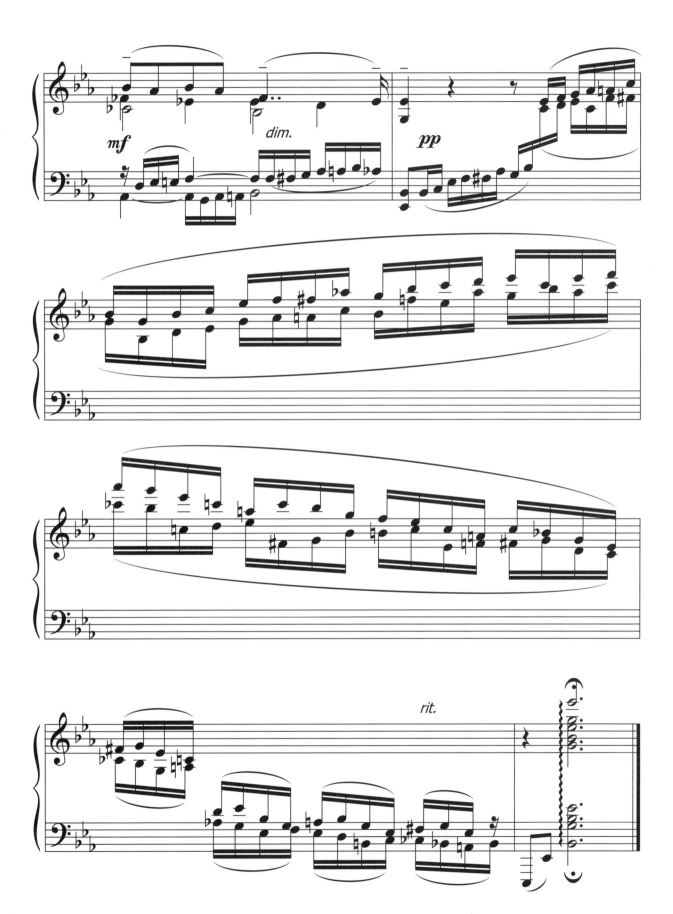

# Prelude in E Major
## (Op 32, No. 3)

Allegro vivace

molto marcato

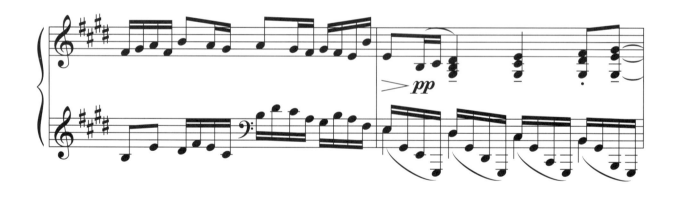

*poco a poco dim.*

# Prelude in F Major

## (Op 32, No. 7)

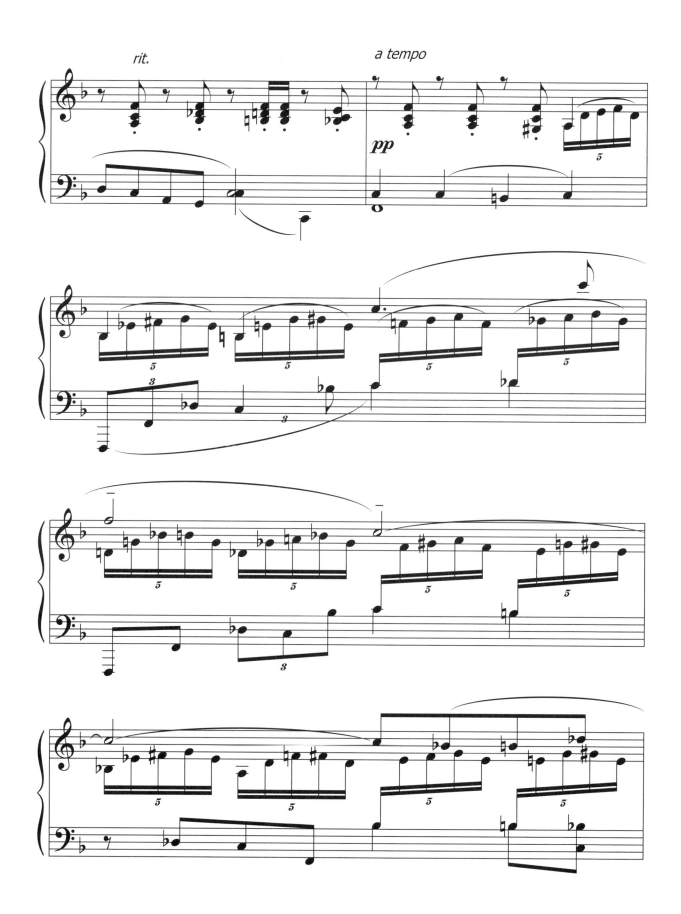

# Prelude in G Flat Major
## (Op 23, No. 10)

Largo

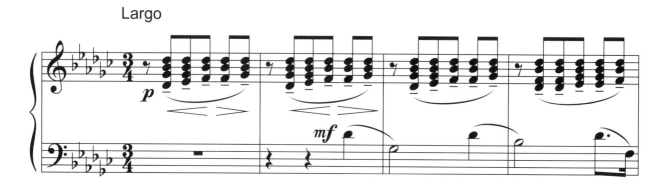

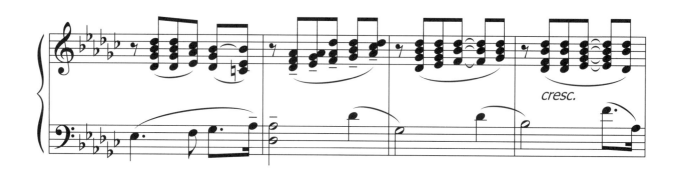

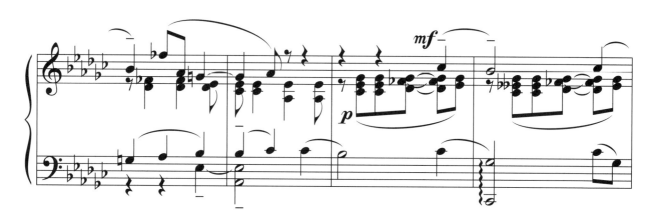

# Prelude in G Minor

## (Op 23, No. 5)

Alla marcia

# Rhapsody on a Theme of Paganini
## (Op. 43, Var. 18)

Andante cantabile

# Romance
## (Op 10, No. 6 in F Minor)

Andante doloroso

# Serenade

## (Op. 3, No. 5 in B Flat Minor)

Sostenuto

Tempo di Valse

# Valse
## (Op 10, No. 2 in A Major)

Allegro assai

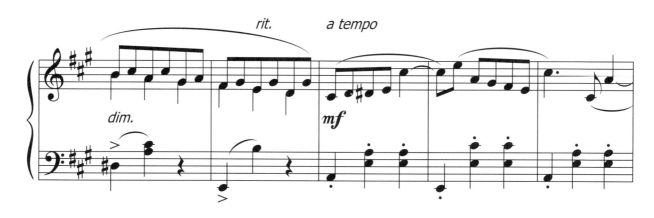

Allegro

# Vocalise
## (Op 34, No. 14)

Lentamente. Molto cantabile

# www.flametreepiano.com

**Audio playlists** with the pieces from this book.

**Comprehensive** biography of Rachmaninov.

**Free eBook**: *Romantic Composers.*

**Resource links** to books and internet sites.

**Recommended recordings**.